I0199551

The Dream

Matt McCarty

The Dream

Copyright © 2020 by Matthew McCarty. All rights reserved.

Published in the United States of America

ISBN: 978-0-9863242-4-6

Library of Congress Catalog Card Number: 2020902728

Acknowledgements

Mia, thanks again for allowing me the
great adventure of writing this book.
You and the girls are my inspiration and support.
I couldn't have done this without you.

Hannah, another job well done!
You always bring my stories to life.

Dedication

This is for every person who has ever stood up for equality.
Our founders believed that all men (including women) were
created equal. My prayer is that future generations
will share the same belief.

In honor of Dr. King, "…let us not judge people
by the color of their skin, but by the content of their character."

It was Saturday morning and Matthew jumped out of bed!
What a funny dream, he thought to himself. He had
to tell Mom all about it, so he rushed downstairs.

Besides, his friend Fred would be over for pancakes soon,
and he wanted to be ready.

"Hey Mom,"
Matthew said, as he poured himself a glass of chocolate milk.

"You'll never believe the dream I had last night."

"And what would that be?" Mom asked curiously.

"I dreamt that I was chasing a peanut butter and jelly sandwich!"
he said with a smile.

"Well that IS a funny dream." Mom laughed.
"But why were you chasing it?" She asked.

"So I could catch it and eat it, of course!" he giggled.

Mom smiled. She thought this would be a good chance
to teach Matthew a lesson about a very special man
who once had a BIG dream.

"Dreams can be pretty funny sometimes, huh Matthew?"
asked Mom.

"Sometimes dreams are funny, sometimes dreams are scary,
and sometimes dreams can even change a nation." She continued.

"Chasing after a giant sandwich IS pretty funny, but how can a
dream change a nation?" Matthew asked.

"Well, did you know that dreams can be shared
with other people?" Mom pressed.

"Yeah, kind of like how I shared my sandwich dream
with you, right?" he asked.

"Exactly. In fact, sometimes sharing a dream with others
can inspire them." she said.

"What do you mean?" Matthew asked.

Mom began to explain.

"There once was a man named Dr. Martin Luther King Jr.," Mom said, "but I'll just call him Dr. King."

"He was, and is, a very famous man. He became famous because of the work he did to change how people treated each other."

"In fact, Dr. King had lots of dreams about people being nice to each other. He shared one of those dreams with a large group of people one day." Mom continued.

Mom picked up a book and flipped through the pages.
She turned it around so Matthew could see a picture of what she
was talking about.

Matthew gazed at it curiously. It was a picture of a man
standing in front of a podium, speaking into a microphone,
in front of thousands of people.

"Is that guy Dr. King?" asked Matthew.

"It sure is." Mom answered.
"This is a picture of when Dr. King shared his dream."
She continued.

She began to read from the book.

"I have a dream," Mom read, "…that my four little children will one day live in a nation where they will not be judged by the color of their skin but by the content of their character."

Mom took the next few minutes to read Dr. King's speech to Matthew. When she was done, Matthew looked confused.

"That sounds like a pretty cool dream Mom, but it doesn't sound funny like my dream did." Matthew said.

"That's true." Mom answered. "Remember, not all dreams are funny. Dr. King's dream was a serious one. He wanted people to change how they treated each other, so he told them all about his dream."

Matthew's mom then began to explain to him how people were treating each other at that point in history.

She told him that sometimes people were mean to others because of the color of their skin. She continued to show Matthew pictures and pages from the book.

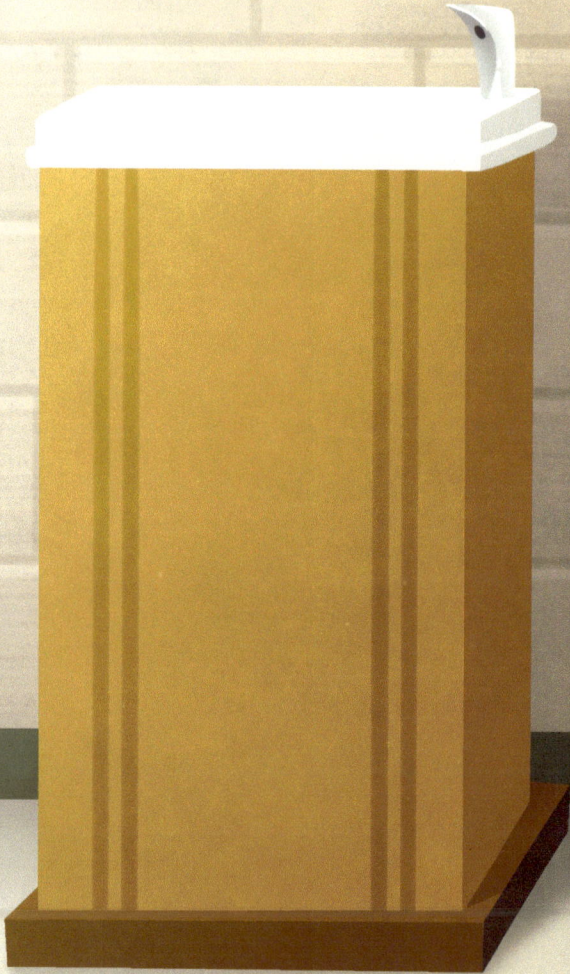

Matthew flipped through it with his mom, as she explained to him what Dr. King's speech was about. Mom taught him that Dr. King worked towards treating all people equally.

She taught him that equality was treating people the way you want to be treated, no matter the color of their skin.

There were lots of pictures in the book. One picture showed two water fountains like the one in Matthew's school. Above the fountains were two signs. Matthew asked about the picture.

"Why are there two water fountains, Mom?"

"Because back then, people weren't treated equally.

People with one skin color had to drink from the fountain on the right, and the other people had to drink from the fountain on the left." She said.

"That's doesn't seem fair." Matthew said.

"Dr. King didn't think so either." replied Mom.

"Not only did people have to drink from different water fountains, but they had to attend different schools, and ride different busses." Mom continued.

Mom then taught Matthew that Dr. King didn't believe this was right. He believed that people should be treated differently based on their character – how they are on the inside – not based on what they look like on the outside.

He also believed that no matter what your skin color was, you should have equal chances to live happily and freely.

"I'm glad Dr. King believed that, Mom." Matthew responded. "I learned in my history class that our country believes that all men are created equal by God."

"You're right, Matthew, and so was Dr. King." Mom said.

Mom then finished her lesson with Matthew by telling him how all the people that heard Dr. King's speech were inspired to change. She told Matthew that because of Dr. King's dream, people started being nicer to each other.

"Because of Dr. King, and many other people like him, kid's that looked different could attend the same schools if they wanted. They could drink from the same water fountains, and they could ride the same busses." Mom said.

Mom then encouraged Matthew to honor Dr. King and all he had done, by treating all people nicely, and equally, no matter what they looked like.

"I'll do that mom. I'm going to treat people the way I want to be treated." Matthew said proudly. "And, I promise to share my dreams with other people too. Even if I'm just chasing a peanut butter and jelly sandwich!" He joked.

"Sounds like a plan." Mom said. "I'm very proud of you, son. Now let's set the table. Fred will be here for pancakes soon."

About the Author

Equality was one of the many things Matt's parents taught him about as a boy. He was taught that America was unique and special because it recognized that all people were created equally. Matt also learned to honor those who fought to maintain that equality just as Dr. King had done. He was taught to express his gratitude to Dr. King, and others, by treating people equally, no matter the color of their skin. Equality is a great gift, and a God given right. Matt hopes future generations will continue the legacy of Dr. Martin Luther King Jr. by judging others by the content of thier character, not their skin color.

Matt and his wife Mia founded McCarty Ministries, which was created to reach youth and train youth pastors and leaders all over America. They spend much of their time investing in the lives of America's youth, and have a heart to reach people with the message of faith. Matt is the author of numerous kid's books that teach American history and values. Matt also serves the men and women of the U.S. Armed Forces as a Supply Management Specialist with The Department of Defense, and is honored to assist them as they defend freedom. Matt earned his B.S. in Business Administration from Cornerstone University, his M.B.A. from Liberty University, and is a graduate of RHEMA Bible Training College in Tulsa Oklahoma. Matt and Mia live in Michigan with their children.

About the Illustrator

Hannah is a digital illustrator and animator specializing in portraits, character design, and concept art. She has animated award-winning short films, illustrated children's books, spoken at events, shown in galleries, and freelanced for over eight years working on projects such as the animated shorts *Overcomer* and *The Land Below*. She is currently based in Broken Arrow, Oklahoma where she continues to freelance and create original content. See more by visiting hannahgraceart.com.

www.ingramcontent.com/pod-product-compliance
Lightning Source LLC
Chambersburg PA
CBHW042026090426
42811CB00016B/1762